The Henry Fords of Healthcare

T0162323

THE HENRY FORDS OF HEALTHCARE

...Lessons the West Can Learn from the East

NIMA SANANDAJI

Institute of
Economic Affairs

First published in Great Britain in 2020 by
The Institute of Economic Affairs
2 Lord North Street
Westminster
London SW1P 3LB
in association with London Publishing Partnership Ltd
www.londonpublishingpartnership.co.uk

The mission of the Institute of Economic Affairs is to improve understanding of the fundamental institutions of a free society by analysing and expounding the role of markets in solving economic and social problems.

A CIP catalogue record for this book is available from the British Library.

ISBN 978-0-255-36788-2

Many IEA publications are translated into languages other than English or are reprinted. Permission to translate or to reprint should be sought from the Director General at the address above.

Typeset in Kepler by T&T Productions Ltd
www.tandtproductions.com

Printed and bound by Hobbs the Printers Ltd

CONTENTS

Nima Sanandaji

Dr Nima Sanandaji is an Iranian–Swedish author of Kurdish descent. He has a background in the natural sciences, carrying out research in biotechnology, structural biochemistry and physical chemistry at the University of Cambridge and Chalmers University of Technology. He holds a technology doctorate from the Royal Institute of Technology in Stockholm in the field of confined space crystallisation. Dr Sanandaji has published more than 25 books on healthcare, innovation, entrepreneurship, women's career opportunities, the history of enterprise and the future of the Nordic welfare states. He is the president of the think tank, European Centre for Entrepreneurship and Policy Reform, and of The Service Factory.

SUMMARY

- Health systems in Western countries are plagued by inefficiency and low productivity growth. Without reform, their funding is likely to require a substantial increase in the tax burden as populations age. Patients may also face a gradual decrease in the quality and scope of services.
- The organisational changes needed to drive costs down and at the same time increase quality and safety – such as economies of scale and high levels of specialisation – have not been implemented to a significant degree under welfare state models. Overly strict regulations and government diktats restrict the ability to adopt radical change. The focus is on controlling healthcare costs over the short term rather than increasing quality and fostering innovation.
- While some of these systems have gradually opened up to private actors, most of the benefits of free markets have not been transferred to healthcare provision. The private sector has little freedom to change systems of health delivery. It is not allowed to use its greatest strength – innovative, disruptive entrepreneurship – to improve the way health services are offered.
- By contrast, developing countries are not stuck in the Western model. The greater openness of health

markets in countries such as China and India has paved the way for the 'Henry Fords of healthcare'. These entrepreneurs show that radical innovation is possible in the sector and they are achieving substantial cost savings and productivity gains.

- The most successful firms are delivering high-quality mass healthcare at affordable prices – something that eludes Western countries. The situation is very much like when Henry Ford and other successful entrepreneurs were revolutionising the process of car manufacturing.

- A common feature of the successful models is their use of an assembly-line approach to healthcare provision, enabling them to capture economies of scale, achieve a high degree of specialisation, and therefore provide a high volume of good quality treatment at low cost. The patient typically comes into contact with one-stop-shop providers and quickly goes through the entire process of care, with minimal bureaucracy and waiting time between treatments.

- Without major reform, it would be difficult to introduce a similar approach in Western healthcare systems. The funding and organisation of healthcare often gives each local hospital the task of treating a very broad range of conditions, making high levels of specialisation harder to achieve. Moreover, healthcare systems are frequently organised such that patients receive portions of care from a variety of health providers, which may limit economies of scale.

- Even though Western welfare states have so far been relatively closed to entrepreneurship, this might change if policymakers realise that it offers an opportunity to cut costs, increase quality and reduce waiting times. Allowing more room for a lightly regulated private sector would encourage the kind of process innovations seen in developing countries. Successful for-profit businesses also have the benefit of being scalable, which means that best practices can spread.

- Growth in health tourism will enable more Westerners to benefit from entrepreneurship and innovation in healthcare, even if regulatory barriers are retained in their own countries. Large numbers of patients are already travelling to destinations such as Thailand, Mexico and India in order to avoid long waiting lists or to save money, and this trend is likely to increase as the problems with welfare-state systems intensify.

- Health officials in the West could encourage trade in healthcare as a means of cutting costs and reducing waiting times, for example by incentivising at least some patients to seek treatment abroad. However, the current welfare-state contract between the individual and the public sector hinders such initiatives.

TABLES AND FIGURES

1 INTRODUCTION

'I hope you become old'. So goes a traditional Persian saying, often told to children. People around the world value the possibility of living a healthy life and reaching old age. We are fortunate to live at a time of unprecedented potential for improving human health.

Breakthroughs are being made in the fields of biotechnology, medical delivery and robotic surgery. Intelligent sensors that can be worn at home as well as in hospital environments allow for detailed monitoring of people's well-being. In the near future, advances in biotechnology will make it possible to tailor treatments to the unique genetic and biochemical signatures of individual patients. In fact, genetic testing and the study of biomarkers already make it possible to assess the risk of future diseases among individuals, opening up new opportunities for preventive healthcare. Growing organs in the laboratory and targeting the causes of ageing – until recently the stuff of science-fiction books – are gradually becoming reality. A new generation of pharmaceuticals aims to alleviate or cure chronic age-related diseases. Functional foods – foods that are not merely healthy in general but have been modified to have specific health benefits – are increasingly available.

However, while health technology is progressing at an impressive pace, the same cannot be said of the healthcare services that are being provided in the UK and other Western countries. Much of the current debate is about how the healthcare systems of European welfare states can improve through marginal changes, such as a somewhat increased role for private actors, or a greater focus on preventive healthcare. While such reforms can indeed have some effect, this book looks at a different approach to the challenge: disruptive innovations brought about by entrepreneurs acting in an environment where they are able to try new health delivery models.

Healthcare is as much about providing aid as about the technologies that enable this aid. Yet healthcare services in many European welfare states and, especially, in the UK are locked in an inefficient centralised system with limited potential for change. Because of this, health services are unnecessarily expensive, shoddy, prone to error and slow to adapt to technological change. For example, a 2015 National Health Service (NHS) report states that:

> Latest figures show that in the six months from October 2014 to March 2015 there were 622,000 patient safety incidents recorded in general hospitals (acute, non-specialist, NHS trusts) in England and Wales. Of these, over 23,000 caused moderate or severe harm and there were 716 deaths – four a day.

Death rates in UK hospitals have long been an issue of public debate. In 2013 Brian Jarman, Professor of Health

Statistics at London Imperial College, found that UK hospital death rates are higher than in other developed countries – 45 per cent higher than in the US, for example (NHS 2015). The lack of patient safety, which still includes cases of operating on the wrong patient, is one of many indicators that the organisation of health services is suboptimal.

A recent study in the *Lancet* (Arnold et al. 2019) compared age-standardised survival rates for seven different types of cancer across seven developed countries. It found that for six out of those seven cancers, the UK had the lowest survival rates (and the third lowest for the remaining one).

Another study in the *Lancet* (Fullman et al. 2018) compiled an index of Healthcare Access and Quality (HAQ), based on Mortality Amenable to Healthcare, i.e. premature deaths that could have been avoided through better and/or timelier healthcare. The UK came out 23rd, which is the fourth-lowest rank in Western Europe. In absolute terms, the UK is about on a par with Greece, Malta and the Czech Republic, and several points behind, for example, Switzerland, Australia and the Netherlands.

The shortcomings of healthcare delivery partly explain why the technologies that help people live longer and healthier lives are only slowly being adopted by the healthcare sector. Because they are largely tax funded, European welfare states are focused on controlling healthcare costs over the short term, rather than increasing quality and fostering innovation. In the US new technologies are more readily adopted. But the US health system results in unnecessarily high expenses, with healthcare spending reaching 17 per cent (!) of GDP, compared with an OECD average of just under 9 per cent (OECD 2019). The health delivery model in the US (where many hospitals and a significant part of the financing is private) is quite different from that in the UK (where most healthcare is organised and performed through a centrally controlled, tax-funded public system). Both are, in turn, different from the social health insurance (SHI) models of the Netherlands, Germany, Belgium or Switzerland, which are systems of universal compulsory insurance, with multiple competing health insurers and typically a mix of public and private providers. These SHI models, meanwhile, are quite different from national insurance systems such as those in Australia, France or Canada, where healthcare is mostly publicly funded, but provided in a relatively competitive setting involving, again, a mix of private and public providers. However, in practice the different health models in Western countries have one thing in common: the organisational changes needed to drive down costs and at the same time increase quality and safety – such as economies of scale and high levels of specialisation – are not implemented to any significant degree. Overly strict regulations and government diktats restrict the ability to adopt radical change.

A paper from University College London and the European Institute argues that 'European governments face a growing number of major health challenges, which are putting unprecedented pressures on public health systems'. An ageing population and patient knowledge of the availability of higher-quality treatments are driving up demand. Since healthcare in Europe, particularly in Western Europe, is mainly financed through taxes or tax-like social insurance contributions, the rising costs are putting the social contract of European welfare states under strain (University College London and European Institute 2012). According to Christoph Schwierz, a researcher at the European Commission's economic and financial affairs directorate, many policymakers in Europe are worried about overall demographics and ageing. If current trends continue, while many Europeans can expect to live longer, they might also experience many years of illness. Schwierz shows that around one in ten Europeans now have a long-standing disability, a proportion which is set to increase further (EurActiv 2014). The healthcare sector is simply not equipped to meet future challenges. In fact, excessive and costly public bureaucracies, long waiting times and inefficient service delivery are already plaguing European healthcare delivery systems (Deuring 2015).

While challenges exist throughout Europe, the UK has particularly severe shortcomings. In the UK most healthcare is organised through the government's National Health Service (NHS). As Niemietz (2015, 2016) has shown:

- The NHS is a nationalised monopoly which, despite the 'quasi-market' reforms in the 2000s, offers relatively little in the way of genuine patient choice and competition (Niemietz 2015: 32–34).[1]

---

1   The quasi-market reforms include the introduction of patient choice, the creation of a new funding system in which money follows patients, the

- Despite some catching up, the NHS still lags behind the health systems of most comparable countries in terms of health outcomes, healthcare quality measures, waiting times and efficiency indicators (Niemietz 2016: 26–50).
- Systems similar to the NHS suffer from the same shortcomings. The models with the best outcomes tend to be pluralistic and competitive, based on consumer sovereignty and freedom of choice (ibid.).
- Since healthcare in the UK is provided free at the point of use, there is little pressure for harnessing technological innovations for cost-cutting, which is why cost-inflating innovations dominate and one reason why the productivity and efficiency performance in healthcare is so poor generally (Niemietz 2015: 44–49).
- The NHS is in an almost constant state of reorganisation, and these – often rather pointless – changes seem to be primarily motivated by a political desire to 'leave a mark' (ibid.: 54–56).

The debate about how to improve health services in the UK and other European welfare states has been going on for many decades. Ideas such as increased spending on preventive healthcare, better use of digitalisation to reduce bureaucracy, streamlining of work routines and pay-for-performance schemes have been suggested as

inclusion of private sector providers and the conversion of some public hospitals into semi-autonomous 'Foundation Trusts'.

ways to improve the systems. Such reforms can lead to improvements. This monograph, however, focuses on the possibility of reshaping healthcare delivery by fully utilising market solutions such as specialisation and economies of scale.

Opening up the existing welfare-state healthcare sector to market competition is not a new idea. In various degrees this has already been done in European welfare states such as the Netherlands and Switzerland, and, in a more limited form, also in the UK. In some countries, such as the US, much of healthcare is provided by independent firms and trusts. However, the healthcare sector in Western countries remains so strongly regulated by governments that true entrepreneurship – the process through which disruptive innovation is introduced – has been almost impossible. While entrepreneurs have been enabled in related fields, such as biotechnology, the development of medical devices and health digitalisation, health service delivery remains so regulated that innovation has been severely hindered.

The barriers to health service innovation have long been recognised. In 2006, for example, Regina E. Herzlinger, Professor of Business Administration at Harvard Business School, explained that while 'medical treatment has made astonishing advances over the years', 'the packaging and delivery of that treatment are often inefficient, ineffective, and consumer unfriendly'. According to Herzlinger a number of different forces hinder improvements in how treatments are packaged and delivered. These hindrances include not only government regulations, but also doctors and hospitals taking the role of 'status quo actors' suppressing efficient and cheap health delivery systems. For example, for-profit actors who provided easily accessible healthcare in US shopping malls were bad-mouthed by health professionals working in established hospitals. This opposition ended what Herzlinger describes as a viable and innovative health solution (Herzlinger 2006).

From a Western viewpoint health entrepreneurship remains a largely untested idea, which explains why it is seldom seen as a viable alternative. In recent years, however, a number of innovative health ventures have succeeded in countries such as India and China. Visionary entrepreneurs have been able to reduce significantly the cost of healthcare services, while simultaneously increasing quality. By introducing market innovations such as economies of scale, high levels of specialisation and e-health, the firms formed by these entrepreneurs can provide high-quality healthcare to millions who would otherwise be unable to afford it. The entrepreneurs who are changing the face of healthcare have gone as far as to introduce the concept of health cities, and are fostering a global marketplace for health exports and imports.

In the parts of the world where these innovations are occurring, a major challenge until recently has been the lack of comprehensive healthcare delivery models. However, this also has the benefit of making it easier to test innovative ways of delivering healthcare. In contrast with the West, entrepreneurs have been able to experiment with novel organisations to meet the challenge of providing high-quality healthcare to people with limited economic resources. The result has been a tremendous success. The new generation of health entrepreneurs who come from countries such as India, China, Singapore and Brazil has created global centres of health excellence which rival or even outstrip Western counterparts. They are attracting significant investment to expand their ventures abroad, opening up hospitals across Asia, South and Central America, and Africa. And their businesses are increasingly targeting Western consumers who seek quality treatments at affordable prices.

And yet, while emerging economies are brimming with innovative ideas for healthcare delivery, in the West we act as if none of this was happening. In the British press, coverage of healthcare-related issues is almost exclusively focused on the NHS, without any references to international experience. The continental European press may contain a reference to a neighbouring country with a relatively similar health system, but this will be as far as it goes. The idea that our staid healthcare models might have valuable lessons to learn from a disruptive healthcare entrepreneur in India, China, Thailand or Brazil is simply not on the agenda at the moment.

This book aims to at least begin to fill this gap. In focusing on healthcare entrepreneurs in emerging economies, we are, however, facing a major limitation, which is that this is a severely under-researched area. The empirical evidence, such as it is, is patchy, fragmented, often observational, and it rarely goes beyond isolated case studies. This is a shortcoming which we are not currently able to overcome.

In an ideal world, we would be able to draw on carefully controlled studies in peer-reviewed journals, which quantify and isolate the impact that our healthcare entrepreneurs have made. We would be able to identify their 'secret sauce' and come up with a detailed policy programme outlining how, and to what extent, their success could be transferred to a Western healthcare system. We would be able to quantify the improvements in health outcomes, and the efficiency savings, that could be achieved if Western health systems adopted a similarly entrepreneurial approach.

However, if we stuck to areas that are sufficiently well-researched to meet such a high standard, we would have to limit ourselves to thinking inside the box. There is plenty of high-quality literature on the effects of parametric reforms within a given healthcare system, but this is precisely what we want to go beyond in this monograph.

Therefore, we have chosen to go for a horizon-scanning approach. We are trying to broaden the debate, and add new items to the agenda, rather than come up with definitive conclusions or a fully worked-out policy agenda.

We are, however, confident that there must be *some* lessons that the West can learn from the 'Henry Fords of healthcare'. If you grew up in a Western country, you will probably think of healthcare as something fairly static. Look up a newspaper story on healthcare reform from twenty, thirty or forty years ago, and you will probably find that it might as well be from one of today's papers. It will most likely be about some relatively minor organisational reform, some change in the reimbursement formula, or some vague references to 'improved coordination', 'joined-up thinking' and 'integrated care'. Chances are that your local GP surgery, your local health centre and your local hospital have been there for decades, and are still doing more or less what they have always done.

But there is nothing inherent in the healthcare sector which makes it so resistant to change, and there are parts of the world where healthcare is not like that at all. During much of the twentieth century and the beginning of the twenty-first century, Western nations have embarked on a policy route in which entrepreneurship has been allowed to change the service delivery model of most sectors of the economy, while healthcare has been heavily regulated and thus shielded from change. Perhaps it is time to change this attitude, by learning from the Henry Fords of healthcare. Their innovative businesses have shown that healthcare provision can be organised in ways that reduce costs and increase quality. These entrepreneurial ventures are playing a significant role in fostering the new market for global health trade which is blossoming, and which is largely bypassing countries such as the UK. Trading health services across borders offers real opportunities for the UK and other European welfare states. Some health services can be outsourced to other countries, reducing costs and creating a better patient experience, while specialised health treatments can be offered to patients visiting from abroad. These ideas have already been tested, and are as likely to succeed in the European context as in India. What is needed is an acceptance of entrepreneurship, disruptive innovation and trade in a field previously dominated by the state.

The innovative ways of providing healthcare described in this book can create better outcomes. Yet, adopting this radical approach necessitates that policymakers are willing to risk changing the system, moving healthcare into what politicians might view as *terra incognita*. My hope is that this book will show that the radical step of allowing true entrepreneurship in healthcare delivery is not about moving into uncharted territory, but rather about being inspired by the healthcare solutions that are already improving the lives of millions of people in the most populous countries of the world. It is time for the West to learn market-oriented healthcare delivery from the East.

2 TRAPPED IN BAUMOL'S COST DISEASE

Historically, healthcare in Europe was provided by private firms and non-profit actors (see, for example, Green 1985). As welfare models evolved, many governments took over not only the role of financing healthcare through taxation but also got involved, directly or indirectly, in organising healthcare delivery. In the mid twentieth century much of Western European healthcare came to be organised through varying degrees of central planning by the state. As with most models of government planning, the system turned out to be far from optimal. During the late 1980s a new, or, more accurately, renewed, stress on the importance of management and production engineering in the delivery of public services spread across European welfare states. The re-organisation trend would be called 'New Public Management' (Hood 1991). According to Simonet (2011) the system 'led to a greater focus on market forces and competition and improved information sharing and cooperation among healthcare networks, and changed the way care is delivered'. Over the years a debate has been raging about the benefits and drawbacks of New Public Management.

In short, the challenge with the system is that it is based on rewarding certain activities. This is done in order to create incentives, which otherwise are lacking in planned economic systems financed through taxation. The risk with New Public Management, however, is that skewed incentives can be created. The services can become overly focused on the precise activity that is being measured. As an example, if the administration of a certain medication is used to measure how many successful treatments have been performed in a certain field, incentives might be created to also administer that medication to patients who do not necessarily need it. New Public Management is thus seen by many as a far from optimal system.

As a report published by Sweden's Expert Group for Studies in Public Economy explains, it might, however, be seen as the lesser of two evils (Anell 2010):

> With goal-based imbursement there is always the risk that the wrong unit is rewarded and/or that relevant goals that are not being rewarded are crowded out. The principles that are developed will never be perfect. Without goal-based reimbursement one can, however, be certain that the wrong units are rewarded since all units are given the same reimbursement regardless of whether they reach their goals or not.[1]

A similar point could be made about the adoption of performance targets in the English NHS (see Niemietz 2016: 68–71).

---

1   Author's translation from Swedish.

The key point is that with or without New Public Management, European healthcare systems are run suboptimally. In the absence of this management idea, hospital units that are performing suboptimally are given the same resources – sometimes even more resources – than units that are performing much better. Incentives to do a good job, and the ability to allocate resources where their benefit is greatest, are simply lacking. Through New Public Management, governments are trying to introduce incentives and foster better resource allocation. This is, however, done in a clumsy way. If introduced properly, New Public Management can lead to some improvements, but not the kind of fundamental change that is needed in healthcare delivery.

Countries such as Sweden, the Netherlands and even, to a small extent, the UK have gradually opened up their healthcare systems to private actors. Although this has arguably resulted in some improvements – such as higher efficiency, the introduction of some innovations and increased patient choice – it is important to realise that most of the benefits of free markets have not been transferred to healthcare provision. The reason is simple: private actors in European healthcare typically operate within politically planned and heavily regulated systems. They have little freedom to change the model of healthcare delivery, besides making minor improvements such as being more customer friendly, introducing minor changes in technology and work routines, and treating their employees better.

When it comes to more radical innovations, however, the private sector is stymied by the state's domination of provision. This is still true even in the more market-based

US model. There are many firms – mainly non-profits – that offer health services in the US. However, their modes of operation are quite similar to publicly run health services. The regulations imposed on the healthcare system hinder economies of scale and specialisation.

Arguably, the architects of New Public Management and of the introduction of private actors in European welfare systems have misunderstood where the power of markets lies. Although these reforms have some benefits, they are built on the idea that small incentives can play a big role even when competing actors have to operate under the framework created by the public sector. A comparison can be drawn with the economic model introduced by some central European countries behind the Iron Curtain: forced by the Soviet Union to adopt socialism, these governments nevertheless attempted to copy market forces by introducing competition among public firms. Although this was probably better than a pure socialist model, it was not an efficient way of organising economic activity. The efficiency that exists in markets is to a large degree about the process of radical innovation, often brought about by entrepreneurs who find new ways of organising work processes. Competition within the scope of systems which limit radical innovation might lead to minor, but seldom large, improvements.

There are essentially two kinds of innovation. The first is one in which a service or a product is improved without being fundamentally changed. This is often done in incremental steps. A classic example of incremental innovation is how an extra blade is added to razors. Incremental innovations can provide improvements, yet the fundamentals of a product or service remain unchanged. In addition, this kind of innovation typically improves the product by adding cost. Such incremental improvements are not to be sniffed at. They are important for long-term development. In healthcare, such incremental improvements of medical technology and operational procedures have led to better health outcomes.

The other kind of innovation is disruptive – like replacing the razor with an electric shaver. Disruptive innovations often lead to cost reductions. One reason people buy electric shavers is to save money over the long run. Although electric shavers cost more to purchase, they last much longer than razors and can therefore be more cost-effective. Disruptive innovations make services and products simpler and more affordable.

As Christensen et al. (2009) explain, disruptive innovation is what the healthcare sector needs to improve in the long term. Yet such changes are blocked not only by government regulators or centrally planned healthcare services, but also by private firms in healthcare. The authors explain that 'in the history of healthcare, industry leaders have repeatedly lobbied for legislation and regulation that block disruptive approaches from being used anywhere until they are certifiably good enough to be used everywhere. This traps the industry where it began, in the expertise-intensive world of high costs' (ibid.: xviii).

A different way of classifying innovation is by distinguishing between 'product innovation' and 'process innovation'. As Niemietz (2015: 45) explains:

> Product innovations are the type of innovation that enables us to do things we were not previously able to do; process innovations are efficiency improvements that subsequently slash the cost of doing it. The invention of the DVD player was a product innovation [...] process innovations then cut the typical retail price of a DVD player from over £200 in the early 2000s to less than £30 a decade later.

Both types of innovation occur in healthcare as well, but the ratio of process innovation to product innovation is much lower than in most other sectors (ibid.). We develop new treatments, but we do not subsequently learn how to make them a lot cheaper over time.

Whichever way we look at it, the conclusion is the same: centrally planned healthcare systems, as well as the actions of private firms within the regulated models of Europe, typically hinder cost-saving innovations. This is why healthcare is often said to suffer from Baumol's 'cost disease'.

This phenomenon, described by economists William J. Baumol and William G. Bowen in the mid 1960s, involves a rise of salaries in jobs that experience no improvements in labour productivity. This occurs in response to rising salaries in the economy as a whole, driven by jobs that do experience labour productivity growth (Baumol and Bowen 1966).

A common cause of alarm for the future of welfare states is that Baumol's cost disease might lead to a need for continuous increases in the tax burden to finance the same quality of welfare services over time. The reasoning is that services such as healthcare do not experience productivity gains, whereas the economy as a whole does. Higher productivity in the economy as a whole increases wages, including the wages of health workers (since these workers might otherwise seek other occupations). Since higher wages are paid for the same services provided, the tax burden needs to increase. Another way of solving the dilemma brought on by Baumol's cost disease is to gradually decrease the quality and scope of health services while retaining the same tax funding to support the services.

A report on the public finances in the euro zone, published by the European Commission (2013), reaches the following conclusion:

> Overall, it can be concluded that developments in current total (public and private) [health expenditure] in European countries since the 1960s are in line with Baumol's theory of 'unbalanced growth'. Wage increases in excess of productivity growth are a statistically significant explanatory variable of (nominal) [health expenditure] growth. This finding is robust to the inclusion of (real) GDP as an additional explanatory variable.

What the report says, in technical language, is that the healthcare sectors in Europe have experienced wage increases over time, not because they have become more productive, but because wages have gone up due to overall productivity growth in the economy. Since healthcare has experienced wage growth in excess of productivity growth, the same treatments have become costlier over time.

This is a worrying development, since the result may be increasingly lower value for every pound or euro spent on healthcare. The good news is that Baumol's cost disease need not dominate the future development of healthcare. The same forces that lead to productivity gains in private service provision – such as digitalisation, new business organisations, greater utilisation of new technologies and economies of scale – can create massive improvements in the healthcare sector. Disruptive innovation is possible in healthcare and process innovation is possible in health-care. This is not just a theory but something that has been proven by a new generation of health entrepreneurs in emerging economies such as India.

3 ENTREPRENEURSHIP IN HEALTH TECHNOLOGY

Can innovative businesses create opportunities to promote human health and increase productivity within the health sector?

The answer to these questions is yes – at least when it comes to certain parts of healthcare. While the provision of health services is largely closed to the transformative power of innovative entrepreneurship, other parts of healthcare are more open. Indeed, some of the most successful entrepreneurs in the world have developed pharmaceuticals, biotech devices and medical equipment. Others provide services such as IT to the health industry.

Christoph Zeller, one of Germany's most successful business leaders, for example, owes his fortune to the company Ivoclar Vivadent. Although the firm's name is not familiar to the general public, its products are used by millions around the world. Ivoclar Vivadent employs researchers that develop new products for dentists to use. Advances in nanotechnology are used to create composite materials for dental restorations which have better surface abilities, are easier for dentists to work with and are more durable than previous alternatives (Dental Aegis

2012). The company has also created an innovative way of using lithium-disilicate glass ceramic material for tooth restorations (Dental Aegis 2014).

This is of course just one example of the many innovative businesses that are driving advances in the field of implants. Another is the UK venture Evodental, founded by dentist and entrepreneur Dr Rajesh Vijayanarayanan in 2008. The business utilises new technologies to allow for total jaw rehabilitation. A feature in *Dental Review* (2015) explains that the firm uses twenty-first-century medical manufacturing technology, the most up-to-date clinical technology and the latest biomaterials:

> Before patients arrive at the centre for surgery, they will already have undergone their free initial consultation and record taking appointment. The Evodental implantology protocol requires detailed clinical and technical planning beforehand so the practice's digital '3D Scan and Plan Pathway' are a mandatory part of the patient journey. Clinicians gather all the information they need to pre-plan and practice the entire procedure in advance on specially developed 3D software.

Many who have previously been told by their dentists that nothing can be done to restore their dental condition are given successful treatment.

Hans Georg Naeder, another leading German industrialist, heads the Ottobock company. This family business has worked with the Paralympics since the late 1980s, producing quality wheelchairs as well as custom prosthetics for skiers, snowboarders, sprinters and others. The firm operates its own science centre in Berlin and is actively engaged in the development of new prosthetic technologies. Together with its Icelandic competitor, Össur, Ottobock has recently announced a philanthropic effort to further development in the breakthrough field of neural-controlled prosthetics. The chief technology officer at Ottobock has explained that 'Neural-controlled prosthetics could transform the lives of thousands of people with limb loss throughout the world, and we look forward to supporting the ongoing exploration of the field through the creation of this new [Össur–Ottobock] fund' (Yahoo Finance 2016).

Joel Gibbard, a Plymouth university robotics graduate, has founded Open Bionics. The company uses 3D printing technology to create bionic arms for those born with disabilities and for hand amputees. The *Financial Times* (2016) explains: 'Open Bionics' bionic arm only takes 40 hours to manufacture with a 3D printer, so the device can be made for just £1,000 – compared with the £60,000 price tag for current prosthetic alternatives'.

The private sector is entrusted with developing faster and more precise dental surgery and even the next generation of neuro-controlled prosthetics. Many innovative firms also sell services to the healthcare industry. For example, Judy Faulkner and Phillip Ragon have each amassed fortunes of more than a billion dollars by founding companies (Epic Systems and InterSystems, respectively) that provide e-services to the healthcare sector.

However, in Western countries the private sector is not allowed to use its greatest strength – innovative, disruptive entrepreneurship – to improve the way basic health services are offered. This is certainly the case in the UK and much of the Western world. In other places, health entrepreneurs have begun to change healthcare through organisational innovations, proving that healthcare can indeed escape Baumol's cost disease.

4 THE HENRY FORDS OF HEALTHCARE

Devi Shetty was born as the eighth child of a family living in the town of Kinnigoli in India. After learning in school about the South African doctor who had just performed the world's first heart transplant, young Devi decided that he would pursue a career as a heart surgeon. He followed up his dream by completing his graduate degree in medicine in India, training to become a cardiac surgeon in the UK and consequently returning to his home country in 1989. Dr Shetty soon became a famous cardiac surgeon, having performed the first neonatal heart surgery in India on a nine-day-old baby, and also having operated on Mother Teresa after she suffered a heart attack and subsequently serving as her personal physician.

He realised that the high cost of heart surgery was simply too much for private citizens and the public system in India to pay. In an interview with the *Wall Street Journal* (2009) Dr Shetty explained that almost none of the patients that came to see him could pay the $2,400 cost of open-heart surgery: 'When I told patients the cost, they would disappear. They literally didn't even ask about lowering the price'. To solve this problem, the entrepreneurial surgeon employed economies of scale. Devi Shetty turned to his father-in-law, the owner of a large construction company, and explained that he needed to create a heart hospital that was big enough so that high volumes could push down the price of treatments. The father-in-law agreed, and in 2001 the new hospital, Narayana Hrudayalaya, opened on 25 acres that previously had been marshland around a cement factory.

According to Dr Shetty, 'what healthcare needs is process innovation, not product innovation'. The interview was given eight years after the flagship hospital opened. The hospital, which had 42 cardiac surgeons, was then performing thousands of heart operations each year. Dr Shetty and his team had streamlined procedures, creating an environment where each employee became specialised in performing the same job over and over again. By employing streamlined procedures and economies of scale they had pushed down the cost of cardiac surgery dramatically. While surgeons in the US typically perform one or two surgeries a day, five days a week, the surgeons in Devi Shetty's hospital performed two or three operations a day, six days a week. The operations of the hospital were continuously scrutinised to find opportunities to cut costs and increase quality. The average price charged for coronary artery bypass graft surgery was just $2,000 in Narayana Hrudayalaya, compared with $5,000 in other private hospitals in India and $20,000–$42,000 in the US. Yet, the mortality rate 30 days after coronary artery bypass graft surgery, one of the most common procedures, was somewhat lower than the average in the US. These figures are quite astonishing, given that many Indians lack access to basic healthcare and therefore suffer from more advanced cardiac diseases when they come in for surgery, as compared with US patients (ibid.).

The *Wall Street Journal* reaches the conclusion that Devi Shetty transformed healthcare in India 'through a simple premise that works in other industries: economies of scale. By driving huge volumes, even of procedures as sophisticated, delicate and dangerous as heart surgery, he has managed to drive down the cost of healthcare'.

Next door to his flagship hospital the entrepreneurial surgeon built a cancer hospital and an eye hospital (ibid.). Dr Shetty has since continued to build up his chain of highly specialised hospitals, attracting much praise for his successful ventures. The National Innovation Council of India has pointed out how Dr Shetty and his team pioneered the concept of a 'Health City', by creating a 'conglomeration of multiple super specialty hospitals in a single campus'. As the National Innovation Council (n.d.) explains:

> The economies of scale achieved through the health cities have enabled the Group to provide affordable healthcare to thousands. He was also involved in coining the term 'Micro Health Insurance' and spearheaded the launch of Yeshaswini, a health insurance scheme for the farmers of Karnataka in association with the State Government which has revolutionised health insurance in the state. The Narayana Hrudayalaya Group, in association with ISRO, manages the world's largest telemedicine programme and has treated over 53,000 heart patients.

As well as the National Innovation Council of India, others, such as the authors of a Harvard Business School case study, have written about the impressive ways in which Dr Shetty has transformed healthcare (Khanna et al. 2005). An updated version of the case study explains how the process innovations adopted by Dr Shetty and his team have benefited the general public, particularly the poor (Khanna and Bijlani 2011a):

> Narayana Hrudayalaya (NH) is one of the world's busiest heart hospitals, where surgeons perform 30–35 complex cardiac surgeries daily. With an average cost of $1,800 per surgery, the hospital treats patients at affordable prices, and does not turn away even the poorest of the poor. The hospital's high volumes provide economies of scale that keep costs low, and offer surgeons greater experience, thereby resulting in high quality. NH utilises its resources, including its equipment and infrastructure, as well as the time of its doctors and residents, optimally, further pushing costs down. The Yeshasvini insurance scheme, conceptualised by Dr Devi Shetty, founder of NH, provides members of farming cooperatives access to cashless treatment in over 350 hospitals across the state of Karnataka.

At the end of 2015, Dr Shetty's venture – now with the shortened name Narayana Health – had 56 facilities, treated 2 million patients yearly and conducted over 300 surgeries daily. *Forbes* (2015) gives insight into how the venture had continued to lower costs and increase quality since the *Wall Street Journal* story was published:

The chain is known for clinical excellence but innovates from the get-go on both processes and materials, leveraging economies of scale. Dr. Shetty has been dubbed the Henry Ford of heart surgeries because his doctors go from one operating table to the next with an assembly line precision that is rare in the Indian healthcare system. Narayana Health keeps tight control on its purchases, driving down prices by negotiating directly with equipment manufacturers like GE and, in some cases, encouraging domestic companies to make in India inexpensive local versions of costly imported medical supplies. Most recently, the chain has experimented with no-frills hospital buildings as well as with patient care – drafting and training patients' family members to administer after-surgical care. All of this brings the cost of a heart surgery to about $800, a fraction of the costs in the West.

In another story, from 2016, *Forbes* explains that Devi Shetty discovered a way of providing high-quality healthcare – better than what most American patients receive – for about one-tenth of the cost typically paid in the US. This is quite the opposite of Western healthcare, where the price typically increases from one year to another (*Forbes* 2016a):

Shetty's methods have been studied by such institutions as Stanford and Harvard. He practiced medicine at Guy's hospital in London before returning to India. Today he is able to perform heart surgery for about 1/3 less than what it cost him in India 26 years ago. Think about that. There is nothing in American medicine that costs less than it did 26 years ago. In fact, you probably can't find a medical service that costs less than it did a year ago.

Narayana is expanding rapidly in India and to other parts of the world. The profitable business is attracting the capital needed to grow. Dr Shetty has explained that although much of the venture is about offering affordable healthcare to the poor, the for-profit motive is important to keep. 'I believe charity is not scalable, irrespective of how wealthy you are', Dr Shetty explained in an interview with the *Financial Times* (2013). 'If you constantly do something for free you will run out of money. You have to look at building business models that are sustainable'.

Devi Shetty is not alone in adopting the process innovations that drive modern capitalism in healthcare. Other health entrepreneurs in India and other developing economies have recently had similar success. Health entrepreneurship on a massive scale is finally becoming a reality.

Another striking example is Dr Govindappa Venkataswamy. The Indian eye doctor, who passed away in 2006, founded Aravind Eye Hospitals – one of the largest networks of eye hospitals in the world. Despite having fingers badly affected with juvenile arthritis, the talented doctor managed to perform over 100,000 eye surgeries. As a young doctor, Venkataswamy realised that many poor Indians suffered from blindness – blindness that could be cured if the right treatment were administered. He began addressing this issue by initiating mobile clinics in far-flung villages. The doctor did this work in cooperation with the Royal Commonwealth Society for the Blind and the Indian government. His main contribution to the Indian public, however, came when, at the mandatory retirement age of 58, he founded the Aravind Eye Hospital. The hospital that began as a small unit has with time expanded to become one of the largest eye-care facilities in the world. A Harvard Business School case study found that the hospital, which was founded in 1976, had by 1992 screened 3.65 million people and performed 335,000 cataract surgeries. Nearly 70 per cent of the operations had been performed at very low cost or free of charge for the poor (Kasturi Rangan 1993).

Both Govindappa Venkataswamy and Devi Shetty were impressed by the efficiency of capitalist firms, and desired to bring that efficiency into healthcare delivery. While Dr Shetty cites Japanese car manufacturing as a role model, Dr Venkataswamy was reportedly impressed by the service efficiency of McDonald's. He sought to transplant it to the Aravind system to cope with the high demand for eye surgery and limited funds to finance it (*Forbes* 2010).

The two low-cost, high-volume businesses are both based on process innovation. Without the efficiencies of process innovation, Aravind Eye Clinic would not have been able to keep list prices at a low level, while at the same time only charging one-third of its clients the full list price. A story published by the Social Enterprise Institute at Northeastern University (2011) gives insight into how the clinic has managed to drive up quality while significantly reducing costs:

Aravind has [...] standardised and engineered cataract surgery for high volume production. About 900 ophthalmic assistants are taken on and trained every year to assist specialist doctors in providing efficient eye care. Recruitment, motivation, and intensive training are all key components that are rooted in making this business work. Dr. V is often routinely quoted for comparing Aravind to McDonald's, the American fast food chain. According to Dr. V, McDonald's' core competency is efficiency and mass production, leading to a business that is both highly scalable and replicable.

India seems to be an epicentre for the new brand of entrepreneurship that is radically changing healthcare delivery. Award-winning Indian physician Azad Moopen started his career as an entrepreneur by opening a single doctor practice in Dubai in 1987. Over the following years, he built this into a multinational chain of healthcare facilities. His business venture, Aster DM Healthcare, operates 16 hospitals, over 85 clinics and 200 pharmacies in the Middle East and India. Dr Moopen, who uses economies of scale through a chain-business network, is investing in highly specialised health units (*Economic Times* 2016). His business employs over 1,000 doctors and covers the spectrum of healthcare consultancy, pharmacies, diagnostic centres, medical clinics and hospitals. It has made Azad Moopen a dollar billionaire. Reportedly, he sets aside one-fifth of his income for philanthropy every year (*Forbes* 2016b).

Yet another Indian health entrepreneur is Dr Ranjan Pai, who heads Manipal Education and Medical Group. The company is a network of 6 colleges and 16 hospitals, run in countries such as India, Malaysia, Dubai and Nepal.

It offers treatments such as comprehensive check-ups, cardiac care, spine care, joint operations, cancer care, kidney transplants and brain surgery. The specialised hospital network is attracting investment from around the world for continuous expansion, and has also made Dr Pai into a dollar billionaire (*Forbes* 2016c).

In fact, two other men in developing countries have also amassed billion-dollar fortunes through health entrepreneurship. One is Chen Bang, who was an investor when he met a retired ophthalmologist who explained the economies of scale in the eye care business. The result was Aier Eye Hospital – the largest private eye hospital group in China. The firm has gained a significant share of the entire Chinese eye treatment market by implementing a similar vision for economies of scale to Aravind Eye Care. *Forbes* reported in 2016 that the group had 80 eye hospitals in operation, and planned to build 200 more by 2020 (*Forbes* 2016d).

A case study by the International Financial Corporation (2015) explains how the efficient service delivery of the hospital network is benefiting the poor:

> Aier adapted a multi-tier network of hospitals to ophthalmology and introduced it to China. The network model lowers costs through efficiencies as lower tier hospitals in smaller cities refer patients to larger, more sophisticated hospitals. Preventative and primary care is conducted through its outpatient department, with services offered in retail stores, community eye clinics and through partnerships with public schools. Doctors and equipment

are shared across the network. A published schedule of tiered pricing reduces corrupt practices by doctors – like collecting side payments or prescribing unneeded drugs. A strong reputation for quality enables Aier to subsidise prices for lower-income patients with higher prices for discretionary procedures like LASIK surgery, which is paid out-of-pocket by more affluent patients. As a result, Aier accepts patients, regardless of income level.

Jorge Neval Moll Filho, Brazilian cardiologist and entre-preneur, has also made a billion-dollar fortune in health entrepreneurship. He founded a health diagnostics imag-ing laboratory in 1977 and gradually transformed it into one of Brazil's largest hospital and lab operators. Today the firm, Rede D'Or, is the largest private hospital operator in Brazil, including 30 hospitals with close to 5,000 beds throughout the country (*Forbes* 2016e). Rede D'Or is plan-ning a massive expansion in the country (Carlyle Group 2015).

There are of course many more examples of private healthcare systems to be found in India, China, Brazil, Thailand, Malaysia, Dubai and other non-Western coun-tries. The point is not that all of them are thriving, or that all of them are creating massive improvements for society. It is that some of the most successful firms are delivering high-quality mass healthcare at affordable prices – some-thing that eludes Western countries. The situation is very much like when Henry Ford and other successful entrepre-neurs were revolutionising the process of car manufactur-ing. Not all of the firms involved in the early production of automotive vehicles had successful business models. But a number of them achieved considerable success, and their business models spread and were mimicked by others through the process of market competition. Similar market forces have recently allowed for improvements in health service delivery, at least in those parts of the world where the health provision model is not stuck in rigid structures.

5 WHAT FORCES ARE AT WORK?

In the Western world, new technologies that are changing the scope of healthcare are given considerable attention. Progress in health technology is frequently reported by the media and discussed by policymakers. However, the fact that a number of visionary entrepreneurs are revolutionising health service provision through process innovations is not widely known or reported. A likely reason is that innovative entrepreneurship in the Western context is associated with change that occurs in established market economies such as Western Europe, the US and Japan. Changes happening in emerging economies such as India and China are seldom seen as something to be inspired by. But we *should* take inspiration from the new generation of health entrepreneurs in developing economies. We should examine what forces are behind these success stories and ask how the same forces can be allowed to improve healthcare in countries such as the UK.

As mentioned in the introduction, this is, unfortunately, an under-researched area. We are not currently in a position to identify in detail what the 'secret sauce' of our healthcare entrepreneurs is, or whether there are common threads that connect all of these seemingly disparate case studies. We can say that these entrepreneurs have all come up with process innovations of some sort. We can also say that economies of scale and specialisation have played a key role. But this is more like saying 'the secret sauce is tomato-based, and it contains some measure of chilli and garlic', rather than coming up with the actual recipe. And yet – we have to start somewhere.

As noted in the previous chapter, the *Wall Street Journal* (2009) has dubbed Devi Shetty the 'Henry Ford of Heart Surgery'. This is a fitting title. He has successfully applied standardised work routines and economies of scale to heart surgery, cancer treatment and other specialised health services. Much like Henry Ford made cars available to the American middle class by introducing the same innovations in car manufacturing, Dr Shetty has made it possible for Indians who could otherwise not afford even rudimentary treatment to get high-quality surgery. In fact, the title would fit most of the health service entrepreneurs mentioned in the previous chapter. So let's begin by examining the innovations of Henry Ford.

The concepts of standardised production and economies of scale were utilised by Henry Ford in the early twentieth century. Although Ford is the entrepreneur frequently associated with these process innovations, they were already relatively well established in the nineteenth century. Ford did not invent standardised production and economies of scale; he implemented them in automobile manufacturing and refined them. Taking an innovation that works in one sector and applying it to another is not necessarily easy. This is why Ford is still admired for his entrepreneurial talent. Still, over time the concepts that made Ford's industries successful have spread to most manufacturing sectors. Retailers such as Walmart and international service firms have adopted similar measures to improve efficiency and increase the value given to customers.

The concepts that Henry Ford is famous for are now commonplace. The real question therefore is not why Dr Shetty and his like have succeeded in bringing the same features to healthcare today, but why this was not done a long time ago. After all, as Dr Shetty himself has pointed out, what makes his hospitals function well is not recent technological innovations but efficient organisational practices that in theory could have been introduced a long time ago.

'Japanese companies reinvented the process of making cars. That's what we're doing in healthcare', Dr Shetty has explained (ibid.). Indeed, the Japanese car companies introduced and refined a number of concepts such as just-in-time manufacturing and lean production. These organisational innovations, which are about creating work-flows free from inefficiencies, were studied by researchers during the late 1980s and the 1990s. They found that the innovations had gradually been developed by Japanese firms over a long period. Kiichiro Toyoda, founder of the Toyota Motor Corporation, played an important part in this regard. Toyoda developed Kaizen in the 1930s – a model through which all employees from the CEO to assembly-line workers continuously strive to improve the functions of the firm, removing inefficiencies. The model spread among Japanese firms after World War II. Eventually, the concept spread to manufacturers and service providers around the world. Thus, when Dr Shetty strives to mimic the organisational innovations of Japanese car manufacturers, he is following in the footsteps of business leaders in many other sectors. Similarly, Govindappa Venkataswamy explained that he based his vision of Aravind Eye Hospital on the service efficiency of – as mentioned – McDonald's (*Forbes* 2010). Again, it is not necessarily about coming up with revolutionary concepts, but rather adapting existing organisational innovations to health service provision.

Why haven't these innovations reached the healthcare sector before? In *Harvard Business Review*, Regina Herzlinger (2006) explains that 'Healthcare – in the United States, certainly, but also in most other developed countries – is ailing and in need of help'. The reason is mainly that the packaging and delivery of health services is often inefficient and customer unfriendly. According to Herzlinger (ibid.) a major part of the explanation lies in the fact that healthcare, even in the US where many health operators are private, has been hindered by regulations from exploiting economies of scale:

> Healthcare is still an astonishingly fragmented industry. More than half of U.S. physicians work in practices of three or fewer doctors; a quarter of the nation's 5,000 community hospitals and nearly half of its 17,000 nursing homes are independent; and the medical device and biotechnology sectors are made up of thousands of

small firms. Innovative business models, particularly those that integrate healthcare activities, can increase efficiency, improve care, and save consumers time. You can roll a number of independent players up into a single organisation – horizontal integration – to generate economies of scale. Or you can bring the treatment of a chronic disease under one roof – vertical integration – and make the treatment more effective and convenient. In the latter case, patients get one-stop shopping and are freed from the burden of coordinating their care with myriad providers (for example, the ophthalmologists, podiatrists, cardiologists, neurologists, and nephrologists who care for diabetics). Such 'focused factories,' to adopt C. Wickham Skinner's term, cut costs by improving patients' health. Furthermore, they reduce the likelihood that an individual's care will fall between the cracks of different medical disciplines.

Similarly, in the UK general practitioners run a large number of small practices. While these practices sometimes do have the benefit of allowing the patient to form a personal bond with the physician, they are too small to utilise economies of scale.

In the Western world, healthcare is organised mainly through either public monopolies or strictly regulated private firms. Much of the financing of healthcare firms comes through publicly funded systems or health insurance that adheres to strict public regulation. These models counteract economies of scale because the political goal is often for local hospitals to deliver a nearly complete package of different treatments. There is simply little if any room for the highly specialised eye surgery or heart treatments that have been introduced in India and China. Of course, a centrally planned system such as the NHS could in theory organise healthcare provision through highly specialised hospitals. But this is typically not the way in which its services are structured. Other Western healthcare systems also focus on the ideal of each local hospital offering nearly all available treatments. This form of organisation seems strongly connected to the welfare-state healthcare model.

Clayton Christensen, a researcher whose work on innovations is widely cited, explains that major innovations tend to be disruptive. This means that they act by tearing down existing structures, rather than within those structures. Much of the inefficiency that exists in healthcare service provision in the West is not about the inability to introduce small improvements in how the job is done, although this might sometimes be the case due to limited competition and lack of economic incentives. The main issue is that major changes, such as introducing a health city comprising super-specialised hospitals as Devi Shetty has done, are simply not allowed by the system (Christensen 2011).

Additionally, Christensen explains that while new technologies are often created by major firms, business model innovations are often introduced by new entrants to markets. This means that a major private hospital might be good at introducing continuous small improvements, but it may still be stuck in its current business model. If genuinely innovative business models that disrupt the current structure, such as those mentioned earlier in this book, are to gain a foothold, new entrepreneurial firms have to introduce them. These kinds of innovations in turn need to be linked to novel ways of financing healthcare. Christensen (ibid.) explains that:

> disruption rarely happens piecemeal, where stand-alone disruptions are plugged into the existing value network of an industry. Rather, entirely new value networks arise, disrupting the old. Hence, disruptive business models such as value-adding process clinics, retail clinics, and facilitated networks must be married with disruptive innovations in insurance and reimbursement in order to reap the full impact in cost and accessibility.

The innovations of people such as Devi Shetty, Govindappa Venkataswamy, Chen Bang and Jorge Neval Moll Filho have been about disrupting old business structures and revenue models. The work of these entrepreneurs is in one regard unexceptional, since they have introduced well-known drivers of efficiency such as economies of scale and lean production into a new sector. Although it is always difficult to revolutionise a sector, it helps if similar changes have already been successfully adapted in other parts of the economy, since that gives a blueprint to follow. In another regard, however, the work of these entrepreneurs is quite astonishing, since they have enacted change in the healthcare sector, which for so long has been plagued by inefficiencies. In fact, as previously discussed, the health sector has been so strongly associated with an inability to introduce organisational improvements that a common theory is that health services are bound to become increasingly costly relative to other goods and services (through Baumol's cost disease). The new generation of health entrepreneurs has largely disproven this idea. They have also played a key role in making international health trade a viable and growing business.

6 EXPORTING HEALTHCARE

Travelling abroad to receive healthcare is not an entirely new phenomenon. The ancient Greeks constructed temples in honour of their god of medicine, Asclepius. These became some of the world's first health centres. People travelled far to these temples in order to seek cures for their ailments. That people can travel to get the best available healthcare is in fact a good idea, at least for specialised treatments and those patients who are able to travel. However, the modern welfare systems of Western countries have been built upon the principle that health services should be provided in local hospitals. Patients seldom go to other regions, and even more rarely to other countries, to receive higher-quality specialist care.

The health sectors of Western countries are not completely closed to the idea of trade in healthcare. As an illustrative example, the small country of Iceland has a deal with the public health system in Sweden. Each year a small number of patients are flown from Iceland to Sweden to get specialised care. And the European Union has a scheme enabling citizens of member countries who work in or travel to other member countries to get treatment abroad. The member country pays the healthcare bill to the country in which the treatment is given. On the whole, however, health trade is not a major phenomenon in Western health sectors.

The reason is not necessarily that those in charge of public-sector health systems are against the idea of health trade. Their administrators have long flirted with the idea of selling health services to other countries, perhaps driven by the notion that their model of health delivery is superior to those of neighbouring countries. However, as is the case for other goods and services provided by the state, publicly financed and organised healthcare has not successfully been internationalised. There are some examples of specialised hospitals in the West. One example in the UK is Moorfields Eye Hospital, a specialist NHS eye hospital in London run by a Foundation Trust. Such hospitals do attempt to attract foreign patients but their ability to do so is limited. The organisation and financing of healthcare in European welfare states does not encourage trade in health. As a result of the lack of trade, even within regions in the same country, Western healthcare has a relatively low level of specialisation. Local hospitals often have to provide nearly all treatments that can be demanded. This lack of specialisation, and therefore economies of scale, reduces efficiency. An analogy can be made with restaurants which have such a broad menu that they fail to excel in any particular category.

Globally, however, health trade is growing in importance. The OECD explains that healthcare provision has undergone a process of globalisation in recent decades, giving rise to new patterns of consumption and production. Patients increasingly cross borders in the pursuit of medical treatments, a phenomenon commonly termed 'medical tourism' (Lunt et al. 2011; OECD 2014). Some European countries, such as Luxembourg, import a significant share of health services from their neighbours rather than producing all services themselves. The new market economies of Europe in particular – the Central and Eastern European nations – are also engaging in health exports on a relatively large scale. Yet, as shown in Figure 1 and Figure 2, even within the European Union system for healthcare of citizens in other member states, the West European welfare states have minimal health trade. This is particularly true of the UK, which has the lowest recorded health exports and imports as a share of health expenditure (OECD 2014).

Country size is an important factor here: it is not too surprising that Luxembourg and Iceland, which are simply too small to achieve a high degree of specialisation domestically, have more internationally integrated healthcare systems than, for example, France or Italy. But the way healthcare is organised also seems to play a role. The relatively market-oriented system of the Netherlands is among the most internationalised in Europe, although with a population of 17 million people, they could, in principle, achieve 'healthcare self-sufficiency'. Even Germany, with a population of 82 million people, purchases a comparatively high proportion of healthcare services abroad.

Figure 1   Imports of healthcare services as a share of health
expenditure, 2012, and their annual growth
rate in real terms, 2007–12 (or nearest year)

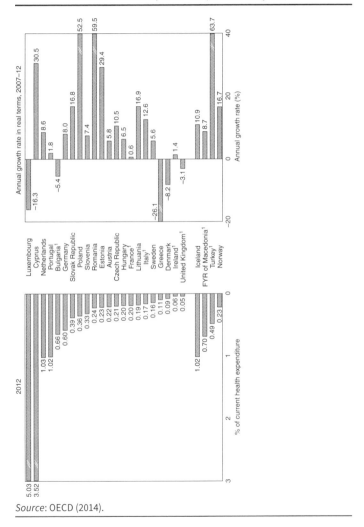

Source: OECD (2014).

Figure 2   Exports of health-related travel or other services as a share of health expenditure, 2012, and their annual growth rate in real terms, 2007–12 (or nearest year)

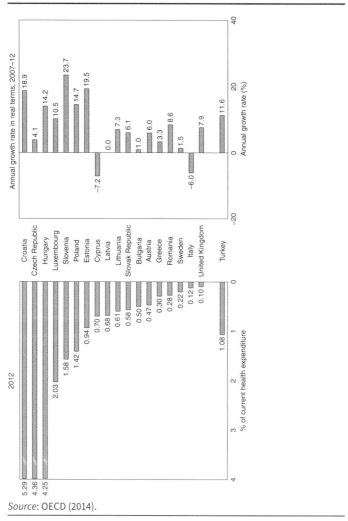

Source: OECD (2014).

There is also an East–West divide. Like India, China and Brazil, the Central and Eastern European countries are not (yet) completely stuck in traditional public healthcare provision models. Their systems adapt to health trade more readily than those of Western Europe. However, due to the limited size of Central and Eastern European countries, none of the major global health trade destinations are found in Europe. Instead they are mainly found in Asia and North America. According to a study by Deloitte (2014) some 400,000 people visited India in 2012 to receive healthcare. This can be compared with about 600,000 health tourists to Singapore, 800,000 to the US, 1 million to Mexico and 1.2 million to Thailand. Although millions of people are already travelling abroad to get medical treatment, we are probably looking at what is merely the start of a global phenomenon. According to a report by Grant Thornton (2015), the market for medical tourism amounted to US$17 billion in 2015. It is predicted to grow rapidly over the coming years (Figure 3).

How can the relatively new phenomenon of large-scale health tourism be explained? According to researcher Howard Bye (2007), the following factors drive people to seek aid abroad:

- To get medical treatments not offered in their native countries.
- To avoid waiting times for healthcare services in their native countries.
- To access cheaper healthcare.
- To buy medicines at a lower cost.

- To access higher-quality treatment.

Figure 3   Medical tourism destinations in 2012 (thousands of patients)

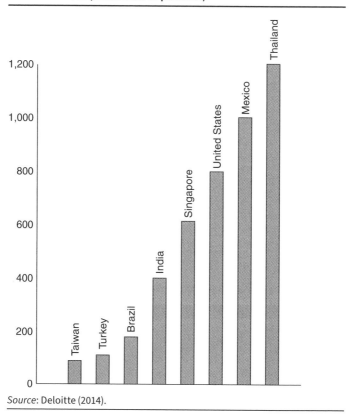

Source: Deloitte (2014).

Introducing a higher level of specialisation and encouraging more health trade will be difficult in the existing welfare-state healthcare systems. Patients and politicians typically oppose the idea of not being able to receive nearly all treatments at the local hospital. Proximity is often mistaken as being more important than quality of care. The fact that healthcare is mainly financed through public and private health insurance, and that such insurance is typically focused on providing healthcare in the local region, hinders the development of health trade. Patients often travel abroad to purchase treatments not covered by public or private health insurance (Bye 2007). This shows that when in the position of a consumer who chooses the health provider and pays for treatment, patients do opt for health trade. Within the scope of the existing welfare-state contract, however, the same patients might very well oppose having to travel to reduce costs, even if the care in a specialised hospital is of higher quality.

Gradually, as health insurance adapts to pay for health provided in other regions or countries, health tourism is likely to become more common. Even though the welfare states of Western Europe have so far been relatively closed to trade in health, this might change if policy leaders realise that it offers an opportunity to cut costs, increase quality and reduce waiting times. It will be difficult, but not impossible, to introduce more health trade within welfare-state systems. Of course, health tourism is not only made possible by the push effect of individuals or health officials willing to seek healthcare abroad, but also the pull effect from entrepreneurial ventures that attract patients to major health destinations such as Thailand, Mexico, the US, Singapore and India. As discussed in the next chapter, businesses in these countries have relied on different advantages for attracting health visitors.

7 INTERNATIONALISING HEALTH SERVICES

The rise in medical tourism has been linked to immigration. For example, Mexican migrants who live in the US often travel home to meet their families and use the opportunity to seek medical care in their home country. Although much of the healthcare bill in the US is paid either by the public sector or by insurance policies linked to employment, the cost difference between health services offered in the US and Mexico is so big that it often makes sense for the individual to seek healthcare in the latter. Those forms of healthcare where out-of-pocket financing is more common, such as dentistry and cosmetic surgery, are particularly attractive for those travelling from the US to Mexico (Grant Thornton 2015).

The quality of treatment in Mexico may in many instances be lower than in the US, but the cost difference makes up for this. This is particularly true of small healthcare providers. However, some major providers in Mexico have focused on attracting visitors by combining low costs with high quality. In 2015 there were nine healthcare providers in Mexico that had been accredited by the Joint Commission International (JCI), thus obtaining a global certificate which shows that they have a high level of patient safety and good quality of care (ibid.). The first hospital to earn this recognition was the private Hospital Galenia. Founded in 1998 by a group of doctors and entrepreneurs, it is focused on attracting medical tourists from the US and other countries (Cisco Technology News Site 2013). The initial pull-factor in Mexico was lower costs. However, as the health provision model in the country has been changed by ventures specialising in attracting foreigners, quality has become a major focus.

Although Thailand lacks the natural flow of patients across a large land border with the high-cost US, its healthcare sector attracts even more visitors than Mexico's. Providers in Thailand compete by offering patients three main benefits: lower costs, a more personal service and the chance to recover in nice surroundings, enjoying good food and beautiful nature rather than the sterile environments of traditional hospitals (Deloitte 2014).

A CNN story followed the host Morgan Spurlock travelling to Bumrungrad International Hospital in Bangkok, where he received a comprehensive check-up that many Americans never experience. The final cost for all the treatments he received, including the travel to Thailand and a pleasant visit at a hotel, was around $4,300. The same treatments would have cost $14,000 in the US. Bumrungrad International Hospital, the first Asian hospital to receive the JCI accreditation, features not only low costs and personal service, but also a number of health innovations. Rather than the traditional and unpleasant method of performing a colonoscopy – wherein a thin tube is inserted in the colon – Spurlock was given a capsule to swallow that was equipped with a camera. The small camera live-streamed video as it passed through his digestive system, giving doctors necessary information while being less intrusive for the patient. The CNN story, entitled 'Surf, sand ... and surgery? Inside the world of medical tourism', explained how those who travelled to Thailand could combine the benefits of low-cost, high-quality healthcare with a tourist visit to an attractive country (Cisco Technology News Site 2013). Much like Mexico, the health sector of Thailand is developing through the provision of services to foreigners. By 2015, 45 health centres in Thailand, including 25 hospitals, had gained the international JCI accreditation. The country attracts many patients from the West, Japan and the Arab Emirates (Grant Thornton 2015).

Some rich countries also attract medical tourists. The most obvious example is the US. Although the cost of healthcare in the country is high, not least due to burdensome regulations, the top US hospitals are still global centres of excellence. Individuals who seek the highest-quality healthcare, and can afford it, turn to them. Some US hospitals have even created centres for health services abroad. For example, Cleveland Clinic, a leading hospital in Ohio, has built a state-of-the-art medical facility in the United Arab Emirates. The healthcare sector in Singapore, which attracts many health visitors for the small size of this city state, is like the US focused on premium customers. Mount Elizabeth Novena in Singapore is an illustrative example. The hospital, which opened in 2012, is based on the idea of offering similar luxury to top hotels in a hospital environment (Pasquale 2009).

In the case of India, the entrepreneurs discussed above have mainly been focusing on patients travelling from one part of India to another. The international pull is also strong, however. The Indian government has realised that while the general quality of healthcare was very low until recently, entrepreneurial forces are creating an upward shift in quality which makes health exports to other countries viable. In 2003 Jaswant Singh, at the time finance minister of India, explained that his ambition was for the country to develop as a 'global health destination' (Bennie 2014). According to the previously cited study from Grant Thornton, the medical tourism market in India was expected to grow from its 2015 size of $3 billion to $7–8 billion by 2020 (Grant Thornton 2015). Indian entrepreneurs also reach global markets by creating health facilities abroad and by investing in telemedicine.

An example is the already mentioned concept of the health city, pioneered by Narayana Health. In 2008 the firm raised private equity capital from JP Morgan and Pinebridge Investments to expand to multiple locations across India. It also set up a hospital in the Cayman Islands, an hour's flight from Miami (Khanna and Bijlani 2011b). In the latter location, specialised treatments are offered at much lower prices than in the US. The hospital, founded in 2014 with 100 beds, is seen by the government of the Cayman Islands as a key driver in the diversification of the country's economy. Robert Pearl, healthcare expert at the business magazine *Forbes*, explains why the creation of this hospital, planned to expand to 2,000 beds, is a disruptive change to the US health delivery system (*Forbes* 2015):

At the end of 2013, Narayana Health was operating 18 hospitals across 14 cities in India. With a laser focus on efficiency and quality, the average Narayana Health cardiac hospital performs 40 heart surgeries a day for less than $1,600 a case. That's about 2 percent of the average heart surgery cost in the U.S. with outcomes that rival the best American facilities. [...] Some [...] may scoff at the idea that Americans will travel to Health City. But if Dr. Shetty can match the performance of his hospitals in India, his vision is likely to be a reality sooner than they imagine. Already, the Cayman Islands' business-friendly government has allowed Dr. Shetty to move ahead with development much more rapidly than he ever could in the U.S.

Another way of exporting healthcare is through telemedicine. Telemedicine refers to a form of healthcare delivery where doctors offer consultation or, through robot-surgery, actual treatments from a distance using modern technology. Since it is a new technology, telemedicine is often associated with developed countries. Yet, as *Business Wire* explains, innovative firms such as Aravind Eye Care and Narayana Health are among the global top-10 vendors of telemedicine. The latter health venture started its telemedicine service in 2002 in order to cater to rural parts of India. Telemedicine networks have also been created by Narayana Health in Mauritius, Malaysia and Pakistan. The firm has with time expanded to '900 telemedicine centres in around 60 countries'. Another Indian telemedicine giant is Apollo Hospitals. This company, founded in 1983, operates '115 telemedicine units across 10 countries, 15 academic institutions, and a research foundation, which focuses on global epidemiological studies, clinical trials, and stem cell and genetic research' (*Business Wire* 2016). Today many Westerners who call customer support or IT support are forwarded to personnel in India. In the near future, the same may become true of health consultancy.

The fact that healthcare services are rapidly being internationalised can create significant advantages for Western European countries such as the UK. This, however, requires that the system is opened up to trade in healthcare.

8 HOW THE UK CAN BENEFIT
FROM HEALTH TRADE

The UK health sector is in dire need of productivity growth. According to a report by NHS England, meeting the health needs of the population under the current system is already leaving the NHS with a multi-billion pound funding shortfall, which is set to grow further (Local Government Association and ADASS 2014). At the same time, capacity needs to grow. A report published by the Nuffield Trust suggested that a further 17,000 hospital beds are needed in the medium term, unless more can be done to improve the efficiency of healthcare delivery (Smith et al. 2014). Due to an inability to meet demand, waiting times are lengthening in many areas of delivery. Social and economic costs arise from the fact that people are not given adequate treatment quickly enough (Nuffield Trust 2015). One way of promoting greater efficiency is to take advantage of the growing global market in healthcare. There are four key ways in which the UK can benefit from this.

Firstly, it can purchase health services from other countries. The cost savings can be considerable. As shown in Table 1, savings of many thousand pounds can be made by undertaking individual treatments in India rather than in the UK. The savings are so high that they can often compensate for the cost of travel. If the patient is able and willing to travel, she may benefit from not having to wait for treatment, from getting quality care with a personal touch, and from being able to combine medical treatment with tourism. Hospital trusts in the UK have already been discussing the possibility of flying patients to countries such as India, thus gaining access to cheaper operations. The plans have, however, been met with political resistance, both to the idea of performing treatments abroad and to involving for-profit actors. Presumably, though, the situation would be very different if some of the cost savings could be passed on to patients, either in cash or in kind. If the patient and the NHS could 'split the difference', travelling abroad could become a lot more attractive, creating a win–win situation.

The second option is to attract specialised highly efficient healthcare units to the UK and purchase health from there. A parallel can be drawn to the health city that Narayana Health is developing in the Cayman Islands, mainly aimed at attracting US patients. A similar health city could be created in Great Britain, or perhaps on the Isle of Man, Jersey or Guernsey, providing care to the residents of the UK. Such a development would, however, be hindered by the centralised public financing of healthcare through the British welfare state.

Thirdly, the UK could export health services abroad, to other developed nations as well as to individuals with purchasing power in countries such as India. Much like trade in goods and other services, flows of health services may run in both directions between two countries. The UK cannot of course compete on costs in the same way as lower-wage countries such as India. Instead, the UK could rely on marketing high-quality care in a number of specialised areas. Again, the structuring of health services through a centrally controlled public system hinders such a development.

Table 1   Cost comparisons between procedures in the UK and India

Procedure	UK ($)	India ($)
Open heart surgery	$18,000	$4,800
Facial surgery and skull base	$13,000	$4,500
Neurosurgery with hypothermia	$21,000	$6,800
Complex spine surgery with implants	$13,000	$4,600
Hip replacement	$13,000	$4,500
Simple spine surgery	$6,500	$2,300
Simple brain tumour:		
Biopsy	$4,300	$1,200
Surgery	$10,000	$4,600
Parkinson's:		
Lesion	$6,500	$2,300
DBS	$26,000	$17,800

Source: Medical Tourism in India (n.d.). Figures are approximate.

Finally, UK health expertise might be utilised to create centres of excellence abroad. This is already happening to some degree. For example, at the end of 2015 King's

College Hospital became the strategic clinical partner for the first Indo-UK Institute of Health in New Chandigarh, India. Supported by £100 million of private investment, the project is the first of a proposed 11 Indo-UK Institutes of Health. The goal is to create high-quality hospitals, nursing schools and medical colleges across India. When fully implemented, the initiative is planned to amount to a £1 billion investment (Smith et al. 2014).

Since health trade is a relatively new concept for Europe, the availability of data is limited. However, we know that total health expenditure in the UK was £146.7 billion in 2012 (£121.6 billion public and £25.1 billion private) (Healthcare UK 2015). UK healthcare exports amounted to 0.1 per cent of health expenditure that year, around £0.15 billion. If the volume rose to 5.29 per cent, the same level as in Croatia, healthcare exports would amount to about £7.8 billion (OECD 2014). This illustrates the growth potential of healthcare exports. Not only would they create revenues; they would allow UK health centres to develop into leading global hubs of healthcare excellence by increasing their volumes and level of specialisation. Health service delivery in the UK would benefit from higher quality and better cost control. Some high-profile hospitals in the UK already pursue this, but the highly regulated and centralised system is not conducive to either the export or import of health services.

By focusing more on providing some specialist treatments in the UK, to patients from home and abroad, and incentivising at least some patients to seek medical care abroad (perhaps via financial incentives), the NHS could deliver better outcomes and achieve significant cost savings. However, for UK healthcare to be of sufficiently high quality to be exportable, and for the system to be flexible enough to commercialise services abroad, entrepreneurship would need to play a bigger role. Additionally, changes to the system would be needed for patients to willingly travel to receive healthcare in another country or region. The current welfare-state contract between the individual and the public sector hinders such a development.

9   HEALTH ENTREPRENEURSHIP: A VIABLE MODEL FOR THE WEST

Innovative businesses can also raise quality and reduce costs in the Western context. An example from the US is Geisinger Health System. The firm, which was founded in 1915, provides care for millions of patients in the state of Pennsylvania. Geisinger Health System enjoys national recognition for delivering quality integrated health solutions and has been listed as having among the best hospitals in the country. The firm relies on Geisinger's Proven Health Navigator, a model that encourages a coordinated primary care approach rather than the traditional model of addressing episodic illness. In essence, resources are directed towards preventive healthcare and at informing patients, so they can make better decisions relating to their health. Since this reduces the risk of illness for those covered by the system, it also reduces treatment costs. For example, a recent study finds that the patient-centred medical homes provided by Geisinger Health System lead to 'sustainable, long-term improvements in patient health outcomes and the cost of care' (Maeng et al. 2015).

An integrated health approach is one form of organisational innovation that firms have used for improving healthcare delivery in the US. Porter and Lee (2013) give examples of other best practices. These relate to private actors that have implemented new process innovations. One relates to lower back pain, a common and costly cause of disability. The typical approach in the US health system is that patients receive portions of their care from a variety of doctors, often in several different locations. The process is unpredictable and time consuming. No single entity follows patient outcomes, how long the process of care takes, or how much it costs.

This can be contrasted to the approach taken by Virginia Mason Medical Center, a private health provider in the city of Seattle founded in 1920. Patients with lower back pain call one central number and can often be seen the same day. A spine team pairs a physiotherapist with a physician board-certified in rehabilitation and physical medicine. The patient usually sees both specialists on the first visit. Based on the seriousness of the cause of back pain, the patients are given different interventions. Their treatment often begins the same day as their first visit. The result is higher-quality care, administered more quickly and reliably at a lower cost. With the new system the clinic 'sees about 2,300 new patients per year compared with 1,404 under the old system, and it does so in the same space and with the same number of staff members'. Organisation of care into integrated practice units thus creates more efficient working routines (ibid.). The NHS has a partnership with Virginia Mason Medical Center, with the aim of learning from this lean culture of continuous improvement and patient-centred care.

Another organisational innovation that Porter and Lee point to is measuring outcomes and costs, not only for the health centres as a whole, but for each individual patient. A pioneer in this regard is The Cleveland Clinic, a private practice in Cleveland which reports its performance in managing a growing number of conditions. These include cancer, cardiac disease and neurological conditions. Another example is Partners HealthCare in Boston, which is 'testing innovative technologies such as tablet computers, web portals, and telephonic interactive systems for collecting outcomes data from patients after cardiac surgery or as they live with chronic conditions such as diabetes. Outcomes are also starting to be incorporated into the process of care, allowing providers to track progress as they interact with patients' (ibid.). Other forms of organisational improvements include creating better ways of paying for healthcare delivery. The payment models can be altered so that incentives are created for preventive care as well as for follow-up care.

The case studies described above show that organisational and process innovations can improve healthcare delivery in the US context, despite the US model's well-known shortcomings. The health systems of European welfare states, focused on central planning and provision, have fewer obstacles related to multiple payment systems interacting with one another. However, other inefficiencies exist within the centralised models. For example, lower back pain is a common reason for disability in Europe as well as in the US. The long waiting lists for healthcare in European welfare states often lead to individuals with back pain not being rehabilitated in time. The result is that the individuals lose the ability to work and function in their daily lives for extended periods, and often develop other health issues in the process.

In a study published by The King's Fund, Ham et al. (2012) argue that fundamental change is needed for the UK system to deliver better care. The organisational approach is simply outdated compared to practice in other services where improvements have already been introduced. The authors write:

> The current delivery model in all providers (hospitals, primary care, community services, social care and mental health) is based on outdated ways of working that result in poor value for money and lack of user responsiveness. If the productivity challenges that lie ahead are to be met, a major transformation in care delivery is required.

Furthermore, they explain that adaptation to new technologies is slow:

> Current models of care also appear to be outmoded at a time when society and technologies are evolving rapidly and are changing the way in which we interact with each other and with service providers. While health and social care services have evolved since the establishment of the NHS, change has been much slower than in other industries such as banking and retailing, where the use of technology has transformed the relationship between service providers and their customers. Experience in other countries where healthcare organisations have

already embraced new technologies indicates the shape of things to come and the potential to deliver care more effectively.

The UK, which has a distinct lack of private sector involvement, suffers from a number of shortcomings in healthcare delivery. Swedish NGO Health Consumer Powerhouse ranks healthcare systems in Europe based on 48 indicators, including outcomes, accessibility, prevention and patients' rights and information. Their latest report states that 'the UK healthcare system has never made it into the top 10 of the Euro Health Consumer Index, mainly because of poor accessibility ... and an autocratic top-down management culture'. Instead it is the Netherlands, a country with comprehensive private sector involvement in health insurance and provision, which secures the top position. In fact, the country has done so for five years in a row. The Index explains that the Dutch system:

> is characterized by a multitude of health insurance providers acting in competition, and being separate from caregivers/hospitals. Also, the [Netherlands] probably has the best and most structured arrangement for patient organisation participation in healthcare decision and policymaking in Europe.

Switzerland, which also has comprehensive private sector involvement in healthcare provision, is scored as having the second-best system in Europe (Health Consumer Powerhouse 2015).

Table 2   Optimism about the future of healthcare, by country

'Over the coming years, do you expect the quality of healthcare that you and your family will have access to locally will improve, stay the same or get worse?'

Country	Percentage of respondents saying 'improve'	Country	Percentage of respondents saying 'improve'
Brazil	71	Japan	23
India	60	Mexico	22
Indonesia	51	France	21
China	47	Australia	20
Turkey	42	Sweden	20
Peru	40	Canada	18
Argentina	39	Poland	14
South Africa	39	Germany	12
South Korea	27	Italy	10
Russia	26	Spain	10
US	24	UK	8
Belgium	23		

Source: Ipsos (2017), based on surveying 18,180 adults across 23 countries, during the period 12 September to 11 October 2016.

Competition and private entrepreneurship in the Western context can, at least in some instances, lead to improved health outcomes. It also results in a model which many people are happy with. As shown in Table 2, a global attitude survey at the end of 2016 showed that 71 per cent of people in Brazil, 60 per cent of those in India and 47 per cent of those in China believed that over the coming years the quality of the healthcare that they and their families received would improve. This can be compared with 24 per cent in the US, 20 per cent in Sweden and just 8 per cent in the UK. While part of the explanation is probably that rising living standards in India and China bring with them greater ability to fund healthcare, the high levels of optimism seem to indicate something over and above that.

Optimism about the future of healthcare is not to be found in the West but rather the East. The UK, which has a universal healthcare model with a high level of state control, ranks at the bottom in terms of optimism. At the same time, it is evident that the process innovations implemented by entrepreneurial health ventures in countries such as India and China are not being adopted in Western countries. Nor are they gaining a foothold in either the US or Western Europe. How can this be explained?

10 NECESSITY BREEDS INNOVATION

Why is it that the Henry Fords of healthcare, entrepreneurs who are introducing radical improvements in care delivery, thrive in developing countries rather than in the West? Ehrbeck et al. (2010) attempted to answer this question:

> Many of the most compelling innovations we studied come not from resource-rich developed countries but from emerging markets. Two factors help explain why. First, necessity breeds innovation; in the absence of adequate healthcare, existing providers and entrepreneurs must improvise and innovate. Second, because of weaknesses in the infrastructure, institutions, and resources of emerging markets, entrepreneurs face fewer constraints (this is one upside of the lack of meaningful oversight, which obviously also has many drawbacks). They can bypass Western models and forge new solutions.

It is important to bear in mind that countries such as India, Thailand, Mexico, Brazil and China are relatively new market economies. It is during recent decades that greater degrees of economic freedom have been introduced in these countries. Many of them have relied on, and in some regards continue to rely on, socialist policies. It might therefore come as something of a surprise that truly capitalist breakthroughs are happening in their health-care sectors, while entrepreneurs in relatively free-market countries such as the US have not been given the same leeway. A key point is that the governments in the new market economies have not created well-functioning and comprehensive healthcare systems. For example, India experimented with a democratic form of socialism for much of the second half of the twentieth century. But since the system failed to create prosperity, universal health coverage remained unaffordable.

Even after India's economy started to grow rapidly following the economic liberalisations of recent decades, the government health system has received limited funds. Since a comprehensive health system of high quality was lacking, something had to fill that gap.

A similar situation exists in Latin America, China and Thailand. The Chinese, especially, have a massive pent-up demand for healthcare. Entrepreneurs are a big part of providing it. The scale of entrepreneurial solutions launched in Chinese healthcare is impressive, due to the large population but also the lack of an already well-established system. McKinsey & Company in China wrote in 2015:

> The pharma industry is looking for solutions to big problems. And problems there will be in China: because of changes to consumers' diets and severe environmental issues like pollution, the incidence of chronic diseases such as obesity, respiratory ailments, diabetes, and

cancer are only going to rise. And they're going to hit China at a scale far greater than anywhere else. Medical delivery is an area that is rife with problems and is ripe for innovation. Baidu, China's leading internet search engine, is already aware of the need to improve delivery of healthcare. Its Doctor Baidu app recommends the best available physicians nearby, based on the patient's description of symptoms. The app can also let patients schedule appointments with doctors. Within six months of its launch, Doctor Baidu expanded to six provinces, covering a potential population of 340 million.

They concluded that (ibid.):

> The best innovation historically occurs at the intersection of big problems to solve, technologies that enable the solutions, and a business model to allow the problem-solvers to make money. While much focus to-date has been on high tech, the internet, and ecommerce, we believe the kind of innovation that will change China and change the world will likely come from the healthcare sector.

Although the need for health innovations might now be less in Western countries, in the long term these systems would gain much by opening up to the Henry Fords of healthcare.

As mentioned, entrepreneurship in healthcare is a severely under-researched area. This means that we are not currently in a position to present a detailed policy agenda, which would spell out what exactly 'opening up their system to the Henry Fords of healthcare' might mean in practice. The answer is also likely to differ from country to country. But we can indicate a general direction of travel:

Allow for-profit ventures and competition in healthcare

In many Western systems, including the UK's, there is little scope for the involvement of private profit-making firms. Allowing more room for for-profit actors would encourage entrepreneurship. Although process innovations can occur in non-profit ventures and even in centrally planned public systems, they are more likely in for-profit ventures. Successful for-profit businesses also have the benefit of being scalable, which means that best practices can spread. A limiting factor in Western healthcare is that good practices exist but do not spread. Regulated systems, with limited competition and limited consumer control of where funds are directed, are slow to adopt best practice.

Allow assembly-line health service delivery

A common feature of the successful models we have been looking at in this book is their use of an assembly-line approach to healthcare provision. This allows for increasing volume, and for providing high quality at low cost. A similar system is difficult to introduce in Western countries for two reasons. Firstly, the funding and organisation of healthcare is often such that each local hospital is given the task of treating a very broad range of conditions. High levels of specialisation, which allow for an assembly-line approach, are not possible. Attempts to centralise care are resisted by public and politicians alike. Secondly, Western healthcare systems are typically organised such that patients receive portions of care from a variety of providers. The assembly-line approach is based on the idea that the patient comes into contact with one-stop-shop providers and quickly goes through the entire process of care, with minimal bureaucracy and waiting time between treatments.

Facilitate economies of scale

Much as in other parts of the economy, assembly-line production can significantly reduce costs. This innovation indeed largely explains the success of the health entrepreneurs whose ventures are the main focus of this book. Economies of scale require high volumes. For significant volumes to be possible those patients that can travel to other regions, or even other countries, should be encouraged to do so. Many European regions and even some countries are too small to achieve the economies of scale needed for healthcare to be as efficient and high quality as possible. However, economies of scale in health provision are not optimised even in the US, a country of significant size, due to regulatory constraints.

Allow a higher level of specialisation among health workers

Healthcare is a highly skilled industry where mistakes can lead to bodily injury or even death. Thus, the sector is heavily regulated and health workers need intensive training. A bottleneck in Western healthcare is the limited availability of senior doctors. A lesson from actors such as Narayana Health is that when an assembly-line approach is taken, individual workers can focus more on a few specific tasks. It then becomes possible for senior doctors to focus on providing consultations, meeting candidates for surgery and leading operations while leaving routine jobs to junior doctors or nurses. For example, senior doctors often do the more complex operation tasks, while leaving the opening and closing of patients to junior doctors. Since the doctors, junior and senior, carry out the same operations day after day, they gain in proficiency. This is quite different from the situation in many Western hospitals, where senior doctors spend much of their time performing tasks for which they are overqualified, including paperwork. Another difference is that in Western hospitals, doctors often carry out a host of different operations, rather than specialising in becoming experts in a small number. Lower-level health professionals can also take on more complex tasks if they are allowed to specialise in them.

Encourage financial responsibility and clinical leadership

In its case study on Narayana Health, the UK-based Good Governance Institute (2016) points to the importance of leadership and the financial responsibility of individual clinicians:

At Narayana clinical leadership is a reality, doctors are accountable for the costs and quality of healthcare as well as the benefits. Clinicians, as well as managers, are focused on financial management. At 12.00pm every doctor and administrator gets an SMS text message with the profit and loss account of the previous day. The high level of standardisation of surgical procedures ensures the consistency of costs. Transparency of outputs and outcomes for each surgeon is monitored, shared and peer pressure creates the incentives for constant improvement. Lower level clinicians are accountable for specific clinical procedures and outcomes, for example nurse managers are responsible for monitoring and reducing the rate of bed sores, while specialist intensive care practitioners are accountable for the performance of the ICU.

Create health financing models with greater focus on individual responsibility

A key reason why truly capitalist models of healthcare delivery have evolved in developing countries such as China and India is that those receiving care largely pay for it, individually or through their employers. Western systems, even that of the US, largely put the cost on others. Niemietz (2015) writes:

One of the main purposes of any health system, regardless of whether it is based on private insurance, public insurance, social insurance, tax funding or some combination thereof, is to protect people from the financial risk associated with illness. All of these systems pool treatment costs and break them down into manageable instalments, so that people face only minimal costs (or none) at the point of use. A health system which failed to do that, at least for serious cases, would not be much of a healthcare system at all. But while protection from the financial consequences of illness is clearly desirable, it does have the side effect of creating a responsibility vacuum, because it separates decision-making from liability.

Niemietz goes on to explain why the price mechanism which creates a drive for process innovation exists in emerging countries but is lacking in developed countries in the West (ibid.): 'Western healthcare systems offer security and universality, but they have not yet found a way of reconciling those achievements with price-consciousness and a drive for cost-cutting innovation'.

For change to happen, Western countries do not necessarily have to completely overhaul their health systems. Public funding can continue to play an important role if the right incentives are created. The important thing to keep in mind is that it is not enough to have a market in health; the market must also function properly. To a significant degree, private firms operating in Western healthcare are bound by regulations that hinder them from implementing basic organisational innovations. They can improve health delivery outcomes only marginally.

Fortunately, the new market economies of the world haven't been stuck in a traditional health delivery model, wherein government interference and regulation hinder process innovation. The greater openness of these new models, and the necessity-driven change in countries such as China and India, have paved the way for what I have dubbed the Henry Fords of healthcare. These entrepreneurs have illustrated the possibility of radical improvement. Thanks to their successful enterprises, we know that healthcare can escape Baumol's cost disease. To repeat these successes in the West, we need process innovations to be allowed alongside technological innovations. The result will be not only cost savings but better health.

REFERENCES

Anell, A. (2010) Värden i vården – en ESO-rapport om målbaserad ersättning i hälso- och sjukvården. Expert Group for Studies in Public Economy, Swedish Finance Department.

Arnold, M., Rutherford, M., Bardot, A., Ferlay, J., Andersson, T., Myklebust, T., Tervonen, H., Thursfield, V., Ransom, D., Shack, L., Woods, R., Turner, D., Leonfellner, S., Ryan, S., Saint-Jacques, N., De, P., McClure, C., Ramanakumar, A., Stuart-Panko, H., Engholm, G., Walsh, P., Jackson, C., Vernon, S., Morgan, E., Gavin, A., Morrison, D., Huws, D., Porter, G., Butler, J., Bryant, H., Currow, D., Hiom, S., Parkin, M., Sasieni, P., Lambert, P., Møller, B., Soerjomataram, I. and Bray, F. (2019) Progress in cancer survival, mortality, and incidence in seven high-income countries 1995–2014 (ICBP SURVMARK-2): a population-based study. *The Lancet: Oncology* 20(43): 1493–505.

Baumol, W. and Bowen, W. (1966) *Performing Arts, the Economic Dilemma: A Study of Problems Common to Theater, Opera, Music, and Dance.* New York: Twentieth Century Fund.

Bennie, R. (2014) Medical tourism: a look at how medical outsourcing can reshape healthcare. *Texas International Law Journal* 49(3): 583–600.

Business Wire (2016) Technavio announces top 10 vendors in the remote health delivery market in India from 2016 to 2020. 12 July.

Bye, H. D. (2007) Shopping abroad for medical care: the next step in controlling the escalating healthcare costs of American group health plans? *Health Law* 19: 30–33.

Carlyle Group (2015) Rede D'Or São Luiz, the largest private hospital operator in Brazil, announces capital raise with the Carlyle Group. Press release, 27 April.

Christensen, C., Grossman, J. H. and Hwang, J. D. (2009) *The Innovator's Prescription: A Disruptive Solution for Healthcare*. Columbus, OH: McGraw-Hill.

Christensen, C. M. (2011) A disruptive solution for healthcare. *Harvard Business Review*, March.

Cisco Technology News Site (2013) Hospital Galenia becomes the first medical organization to deploy Cisco medical-grade network in the Yucatan Peninsula. 7 July 2014.

CNN (2015) Surf, sand ... and surgery? Inside the world of medical tourism. 6 February.

Deloitte (2014) 2014 Global life sciences outlook – resilience and reinvention in a changing marketplace.

Dental Aegis (2012) Ivoclar Vivadent composites ensure patient benefits. *Compendium of Continuing Education in Dentistry* 33(4): 298.

Dental Aegis (2014) IPS e.max CAD abutments among new innovations from Ivoclar Vivadent. *Compendium of Continuing Education in Dentistry* 35(2): 128.

Dental Review (2015) Evodental, faster, more precise implantology. 2 December.

Deuring, D. (2015) Europe's healthcare systems face reform to meet growing challenges. United Europe, 10 March.

Economic Times (2016) Aster DM Healthcare to invest Rs 600 crore in Kerala in 3 years. 14 June.

Ehrbeck, T., Henke, N. and Kibasi, T. (2010) The emerging market in healthcare innovation. *McKinsey Quarterly*, May.

European Commission (2013) Report on public finances in EMU 2013. European Economy 4/2013.

EurActiv (2014) European healthcare 'not equipped' to meet future challenges. 16 April.

Financial Times (2013) Corporate responsibility: from the heart. 21 March.

Financial Times (2016) British entrepreneurs seek to use technology as force for good. 4 January.

Forbes (2010) McDonald's and Dr. V. 5 March.

Forbes (2014) Offshoring American healthcare: higher quality at lower costs? 27 March.

Forbes (2015) Devi Shetty, who put heart surgeries within reach of India's poor, is taking Narayana Chain public. 16 December.

Forbes (2016a) Better care at one tenth the cost. 2 March.

Forbes (2016b) #1198 Azad Moopen. List of world billionaires.

Forbes (2016c) #1067 Ranjan Pai. List of world billionaires.

Forbes (2016d) #854 Chen Bang. List of world billionaires.

Forbes (2016e) #569 Jorge Moll Filho. List of world billionaires.

Fullman, N., Lozano, R., Murray, C., Yearwood, J., Barber, R., Chalek, J., Eldrenkamp, E. and Shields, C. (2018) Measuring performance on the healthcare access and quality index for 195 countries and territories and selected subnational locations: a systematic analysis from the Global Burden of Disease Study 2016. *Lancet* 391(10136): 2236–71.

Good Governance Institute (2016) Narayana Health case study, 23 August.

Grant Thornton (2015) Transformative evolution: from 'wellness' to 'medical wellness' tourism in Kerala (https://www.grant

thornton.in/globalassets/1.-member-firms/india/assets/ pdfs/grant_thornton_report-transformative_evolution.pdf).

Green, D. (1985) *Working-Class Patients and the Medical Establishment. Self-help in Britain from the 19th Century to 1948.* Farnham: Gower Publishing.

Guardian (2013) Hospital death rates in England 45% higher than in US, report finds. 12 September.

Ham, C., Dixon, A. and Brooke, B. (2012) Transforming the delivery of health and social care – the case for fundamental change. London: The King's Fund.

Health Consumer Powerhouse (2015) Euro Health Consumer Index 2015.

Healthcare UK (2015) India and the UK establish a strategic partnership in healthcare. 17 November.

Herzlinger, R. E. (2006) Why innovation in healthcare is so hard. *Harvard Business Review*, May.

Hood, C. (1991) A public management for all seasons? *Public Administration* 69(1): 3–19.

Independent (2013) Up to 20 NHS trusts seeking healthcare deals in India. 22 August.

International Finance Corporation (2015) Preventing blindness in China: the story of Aier Eye Hospital. 12 March.

Ipsos (2017) Global Trends Survey (https://www.ipsosglobal trends.com/).

Kasturi Rangan, V. (1993) Aravind Eye Hospital, Madurai, India. In service for sight, April.

Khanna, T. and Bijlani, T. (2011a) Narayana Hrudayalaya Heart Hospital. Harvard Business School Case Study, September.

Khanna, T. and Bijlani, T. (2011b) Expansion at Narayana Hrudayalaya. Harvard Business School Case Study, September.

Khanna, T., Kasturi Rangan, V. and Manocaran, M. (2005) Narayana Hrudayalaya Heart Hospital: cardiac care for the poor (A). Harvard Business School Case Study, June.

Local Government Association and ADASS (2014) Adult social care funding: 2014 state of the nation report.

Lunt, N., Smith, R., Exworthy, M., Green, S. T., Horsfall, D. and Mannion, R. (2011) *Medical Tourism: Treatments, Markets and Health System Implications: A Scoping Review*. Paris: OECD.

Maeng, D. D., Khan, N., Tomcavage, J., Graf, T. R., Davis, G. E. and Steele, G. D. (2015) Reduced acute inpatient care was largest savings component of Geisinger Health System's patient-centered medical home. *Health Affairs* 34(4): 636–44.

McKinsey and Company China (2015) Why China's next big innovation could be in healthcare. China Point blog.

Medical Tourism in India (n.d.) Cost comparisions on some major procedure between India and US (http://www.indian-medical-tourism.com/medical-tourism-india-price-benefits.html).

National Innovation Council of India (n.d.) Dr. Devi Prasad Shetty.

NHS (2015) Organisation patient safety incident reports, 1 October 2014 – 31 March 2015. 23 September.

Niemietz, K. (2016) *Universal Healthcare Without the NHS. Towards a Patient-Centred Health System*. London: Institute of Economic Affairs.

Niemietz, K. (2015) *Diagnosis: Overrated – An Analysis of the Structural Flaws in the NHS*. London: Institute of Economic Affairs.

Nuffield Trust (2015) Health and social care priorities for the Government 2015–2020.

OECD (2014) Trade in health services. In *Health at a Glance: Europe 2014*. Paris: OECD.

OECD (2019) *Health Expenditure and Financing*. Paris: OECD (OECD.Stat: https://stats.oecd.org/).

Office for National Statistics (2015) Expenditure on healthcare in the UK: 2013.

Pasquale, F. (2009) Access to medicine in an era of fractal inequality. *Annals of Health Law* 19: 269–310.

Porter, M. E. and Lee, T. H. (2013) The strategy that will fix healthcare. *Harvard Business Review*, October.

Simonet, D. (2011) The new public management theory and the reform of European healthcare systems: an international comparative perspective. *International Journal of Public Administration* 34(12): 815–26.

Smith, P., McKeon, A., Blunt, I. and Edwards, N. (2014) *NHS Hospitals under Pressure: Trends in Acute Activity up to 2022*. London: Nuffield Trust.

Social Enterprise Institute at Northeastern University (2011) Aravind Eye Care System. 28 October.

University College London and the European Institute (2012) The future of healthcare in Europe.

Wall Street Journal (2009) The Henry Ford of heart surgery. 25 November.

Yahoo Finance (2016) Global prosthetics leaders Össur and Ottobock partner on historic research trust fund at the University of Iceland. 25 January.

ABOUT THE IEA

The Institute is a research and educational charity (No. CC 235 351), limited by guarantee. Its mission is to improve understanding of the fundamental institutions of a free society by analysing and expounding the role of markets in solving economic and social problems.

The IEA achieves its mission by:

- a high-quality publishing programme
- conferences, seminars, lectures and other events
- outreach to school and college students
- brokering media introductions and appearances

The IEA, which was established in 1955 by the late Sir Antony Fisher, is an educational charity, not a political organisation. It is independent of any political party or group and does not carry on activities intended to affect support for any political party or candidate in any election or referendum, or at any other time. It is financed by sales of publications, conference fees and voluntary donations.

In addition to its main series of publications, the IEA also publishes (jointly with the University of Buckingham), *Economic Affairs*.

The IEA is aided in its work by a distinguished international Academic Advisory Council and an eminent panel of Honorary Fellows. Together with other academics, they review prospective IEA publications, their comments being passed on anonymously to authors. All IEA papers are therefore subject to the same rigorous independent refereeing process as used by leading academic journals.

IEA publications enjoy widespread classroom use and course adoptions in schools and universities. They are also sold throughout the world and often translated/reprinted.

Since 1974 the IEA has helped to create a worldwide network of 100 similar institutions in over 70 countries. They are all independent but share the IEA's mission.

Views expressed in the IEA's publications are those of the authors, not those of the Institute (which has no corporate view), its Managing Trustees, Academic Advisory Council members or senior staff.

Members of the Institute's Academic Advisory Council, Honorary Fellows, Trustees and Staff are listed on the following page.

The Institute gratefully acknowledges financial support for its publications programme and other work from a generous benefaction by the late Professor Ronald Coase.

Financial Stability without Central Banks
George Selgin, Kevin Dowd and Mathieu Bédard
ISBN 978-0-255-36752-3; £10.00

Against the Grain: Insights from an Economic Contrarian
Paul Ormerod
ISBN 978-0-255-36755-4; £15.00

Ayn Rand: An Introduction
Eamonn Butler
ISBN 978-0-255-36764-6; £12.50

Capitalism: An Introduction
Eamonn Butler
ISBN 978-0-255-36758-5; £12.50

Opting Out: Conscience and Cooperation in a Pluralistic Society
David S. Oderberg
ISBN 978-0-255-36761-5; £12.50

Getting the Measure of Money: A Critical Assessment of UK Monetary Indicators
Anthony J. Evans
ISBN 978-0-255-36767-7; £12.50

Socialism: The Failed Idea That Never Dies
Kristian Niemietz
ISBN 978-0-255-36770-7; £17.50

Top Dogs and Fat Cats: The Debate on High Pay
Edited by J. R. Shackleton
ISBN 978-0-255-36773-8; £15.00

School Choice around the World … And the Lessons We Can Learn
Edited by Pauline Dixon and Steve Humble
ISBN 978-0-255-36779-0; £15.00

School of Thought: 101 Great Liberal Thinkers
Eamonn Butler
ISBN 978-0-255-36776-9; £12.50

Raising the Roof: How to Solve the United Kingdom's Housing Crisis
Edited by Jacob Rees-Mogg and Radomir Tylecote
ISBN 978-0-255-36782-0; £12.50

How Many Light Bulbs Does It Take to Change the World?
Matt Ridley and Stephen Davies
ISBN 978-0-255-36785-1; £10.00

Other IEA publications

Comprehensive information on other publications and the wider work of the IEA can be found at www.iea.org.uk. To order any publication please see below.

Personal customers

Orders from personal customers should be directed to the IEA:

Clare Rusbridge
IEA
2 Lord North Street
FREEPOST LON10168
London SW1P 3YZ
Tel: 020 7799 8911, Fax: 020 7799 2137
Email: sales@iea.org.uk

Trade customers

All orders from the book trade should be directed to the IEA's distributor:

NBN International (IEA Orders)
Orders Dept.
NBN International
10 Thornbury Road
Plymouth PL6 7PP
Tel: 01752 202301, Fax: 01752 202333
Email: orders@nbninternational.com

IEA subscriptions

The IEA also offers a subscription service to its publications. For a single annual payment (currently £42.00 in the UK), subscribers receive every monograph the IEA publishes. For more information please contact:

Clare Rusbridge
Subscriptions
IEA
2 Lord North Street
FREEPOST LON10168
London SW1P 3YZ
Tel: 020 7799 8911, Fax: 020 7799 2137
Email: crusbridge@iea.org.uk